MAMA

MAMA

ZUZANA PLESA

atmosphere press

This book is dedicated to my mother
and all other mothers

ANNA JOZEFEK PLESA
JUNE 15, 1917–JANUARY 4, 2001

And to Ralph Robert Henson, who
passed away on March 6, 2024.

INTRODUCTION

The mother/daughter relationship is the key to raising a healthy adult daughter. As a counselor, I encountered many clients who have mother/daughter relationship problems, and this led me to examine my relationship with my mother to better help me understand her and our relationship. In writing this book, I reviewed my mother's background in order to understand what was behind her behavior. Writing this book allowed me to have a deeper understanding of what my clients were experiencing and to help them be better mothers to themselves. Holding on to anger and trying to change mother is not the answer; practicing self-care is a better solution. Forgiving mother instead of blaming mother is a more constructive practice for the adult daughter. Reviewing my mother's background helped me to forgive my early negative experiences and to see the positive aspects of our relationship. The biological mother doesn't have to be the one who is the mother connection; any woman who accepts you and is able to mirror you may fill this role.

I had the gift of meeting in Zurich and working with Dr. Kathrin Asper, a Jungian Analyst who taught me how to be a good mother to myself. I quote from her book, *The Abandoned Child Within*, because it gave me so much help and meaning. She gave us a gift in writing this book and I encourage others to read it. I encourage anyone who has had a difficult relationship with their mother to seek help with personal issues instead of denying and burying the anger. We can be healthy adults despite our early backgrounds, but it takes work and sometimes long-term therapy. Seek the appropriate care you need to live a healthy and productive life.

DEATH

On January 4, 2001, the phone rang at midnight to inform me that my mother, Anna, had died. It was not a surprise, but hearing about her death was not easy. I was the assistant principal at Mahan American High School on base in Iceland and had just returned from visiting my mother in Massachusetts at the nursing home. Now I had to make arrangements to fly back to the States. I waited until morning to inform my principal that I had to go on emergency leave to my mother's funeral. I went to the airport and boarded the first plane that was going to the States. I flew to Baltimore, Maryland, and then took the train to New York City. My sister took the train from Massachusetts, and we met at the funeral parlor, which was located in mid-Manhattan. We talked with the funeral director regarding the funeral arrangements and the burial at Linden Hill Cemetery in Brooklyn. The funeral home was run by a Slovak family and near it used to be a Slovak restaurant where we had my father's post-funeral lunch. My mother really enjoyed the Slovak restaurant's decor and food. Both my mother and father had birthday celebrations there. They even played Slovak music. The Slovak restaurant was no longer in operation because most of the Slovaks had moved out of the area. We were so disappointed. We went to a nearby German restaurant and booked it for the post-funeral lunch. I was so thankful that I could make the arrangements with my sister because I was grieving my mother's death and was not in a state to make good decisions. Having my sister by my side was a gift to me. My sister Betty explained the events preceding and following my mother's death. She was visiting my mother on the evening of January 4, at the nursing home. She said good night and returned home. After a few minutes, the phone rang.

The nurse called and said, "I am sorry to inform you that your mother just passed away."

Through tears, my sister replied, "I just left, and she seemed okay, and now you are telling me that she died? I am shocked."

The nurse replied, "I am sorry for your loss. Please come back to the nursing home and we will help you make the arrangements for your mother's body."

My sister, her spouse, and my nephew drove to the nursing home to make the arrangements to fly my mother's body to New York City. The church where she was married was where the funeral was held. She had lived in New York until she came to live with me in Germany before I moved to Iceland. We have a family plot in Brooklyn, New York, where my grandmother, great-grandmother, and father are buried. My mother wanted to be buried with my father, so her wish was granted. I used to go to the cemetery with my mother to visit the family graves. We planted flowers there and made the graves look attractive so the dead would lie in beauty.

At her wake, several of her friends and cousins were in attendance. There were quite a few people at the wake, many of whom I had not seen in years. It was good to see old friends and family. They expressed their sympathy for our loss, and I was grateful that they came to the wake to share our loss. I wrote the following for my mother on the plane from Iceland and read it at the wake.

Dear Mama,

Now that you have left your earthly home, we must rely on memories to sustain us. Thank you for all the stories you read to me about the birds, bees, and trees, and for the pictures you drew for me. It wasn't until later in life that I began to appreciate your artistic talent. Thank you for my sister who became our bundle of joy. I remember all the salads you made and how delicately and precisely you cut each vegetable you placed in the mixture. Thank you for all the crocheted hats, shawls, and gloves that your hands created. They serve me well in Iceland. You shared six years with me in Stuttgart, Germany, and we laughed a lot. Thank you for reading all the signs as we traveled to Vrbovce, Slovakia, the land of our ancestors. Your strength to endure the difficult and incomprehensible happenings in your life provides a model for the daughters who now have the task to continue your values and carry out your mission of service to others. As you leave your earthly home, may your spirit unite with the Spirit of your Creator in eternal peace. Rest assured that you will be remembered lovingly by your daughters.

After the reading, I sat down with sadness but also with satisfaction that I could find parting words to share with and about Mama. With her gray hair combed in a short bob, the natural beauty of her face could be seen. The blue blouse and skirt that my sister had selected for her gave her a modern fashion appearance. Her blue shoes matched her outfit. She could have been ready for a fashion show. My mother liked to dress up and look fashionable, so in the casket she looked as if she were ready for Sunday morning church service. The only item that was missing was a hat. My mother never attended church without a hat. Maybe she wasn't really ready to die but instead ready for church. Are we ever ready to die and go into the unknown?

The funeral was the next day at Holy Trinity Slovak Lutheran Church, which was our ancestral church. It is located in lower Manhattan on East 20th Street. I looked around the church and my heart sank. There were only a few family members at the funeral since most of my mother's family had died before her, including her two younger sisters. It was just me and my sister's immediate family. We are a small family, so it is natural to have few family members at the funeral. My mother had one grandson who was twenty-four at the time and one granddaughter who was twenty-two. They were both in attendance. The cousins who attended were from my father's side of the family. My cousin Olga and her husband Don attended as well as my cousin Paul. Paul and Olga were the children of my father's older brother. Olga was one of my favorite cousins because she always made my mother and me feel like part of the family. I should have been happy with the people who were there, but I wasn't. Where were all the people she had befriended? I was disappointed to see so few so-called friends at the funeral. She deserved better. I thought, *This is the way it is going to be for me too.* She had done so much for so many people and yet none of them were at the funeral. People forget who you are once you cannot serve their purposes. I hope she found her peace in death and resurrection. I wish I had known my mother better and I wish she had known me better. What were her hopes, dreams, and disappointments? What goals was I to carry on since she did not achieve them? Understand, forgive, and love are three key words that helped me pave a new relationship with Mama.

After the funeral, sad memories of my early life kept cropping up like weeds in a beautiful garden. Being an only child for the first nine years of my life was lonely. I longed to play with other children my age, but instead I had to stay at home and help my mother clean the apartment. The cleaning had to be done before I could go out to play, but there was so much cleaning. There really seemed to be no time for play. I didn't have a room of my own to clean, so instead I had to clean the kitchen, which entailed scrubbing the sink and mopping the floor. I also had to clean the bathroom. Scrubbing the bathroom floor on my knees with a brush and pail made me feel like Cinderella. My mother even expected me to dust rugs. I had to carry them to the roof of the apartment building and dust them with a whisk broom. Carrying rugs up two flights of stairs to the roof was a difficult task for a seven-year-old.

One time, my mother and I went up to the roof to dust the rugs. My best friend's mother came to visit and of course we did not answer the unheard doorbell. She later telephoned and asked why we did not answer the bell. She did not believe that we were on the roof, so she forbade Helen from playing with or seeing me. I was heartbroken. Helen had been my best friend since kindergarten and now she was dead to me. Helen had dark hair and beautiful brown eyes. She was Greek-American, and her mother made delicious Greek meals such as lamb with a sour cream sauce. Her homemade gyros were my favorite. Helen's father owned a Greek restaurant, and we sometimes went there for chicken and Greek-style potatoes for lunch. We played house and had tea parties with our dolls.. Helen, being an obedient daughter, listened and obeyed her dominant and overbearing mother. I missed my friendship with Helen and cried at not being able to spend time with her between seventh and twelfth grade. Oh, how I missed my best friend. Finally, at the end of high school, Helen's mother relented, and we resumed our friendship. That was a happy day for me. We talked about relationships with boys and once again ate Greek meals. We tried on makeup and lipstick and pretended we were movie stars. We both liked Debbie Reynolds.

In high school, I still had to dust the rugs and clean the kitchen, and I also had to dust the furniture in all the rooms. My mother would run her finger over the furniture to show me the areas I'd missed. She did not commend me for the areas that were cleaned. Once when I had some friends over, they noticed some dust on my record player and pointed it out to me. My mother heard this and said, "You should be ashamed of yourself for doing such a poor job of dusting." I felt embarrassed and thought that my friends would never come over again. I would be friendless all my life. I wanted to hide in a corner and never come out again. After doing all my assigned tasks to my mother's satisfaction, I could play with my two cousins who lived on the floor below us in the same apartment building. Their mother was my mother's younger sister. I wondered why they never had to do as much work as I did. Of course, I could not question that because I would be considered rude and disrespectful. I did not always like being around my cousins because I felt that they had each other and I had no siblings. At times, I felt that it was the two of them against me. Lillian was six months older than me, and she did very well in school. She also could draw well, and I could not. She was her mother's darling child who could do no wrong. Her brother Bill was eight months younger than me and he was kind to me except when he took his sister's side. Their parents did not discipline them very much, yet my mother tried to make me the perfectly obedient child. I felt that I became rather robotic instead of being able to allow a child's creativity and curiosity to emerge. Later in life, after several years of personal therapy, the child finally started to emerge and blossom. People wondered where the creativity had been hiding. I had to hide my real self to keep my mother's wrath at a distance.

One day, my cousins and I were playing in the park, and I was wearing a pretty ring with a green stone in it that my mother had given me.

My cousin Lillian said, "Give me your ring so I can hold it with my teeth and run with it."

I said, "No, you'll lose it and I'll get in trouble with my mother."

She said, "If you don't give it to me, I'll beat you up."

I was scared because she was bigger than me and so I reluctantly gave her the ring. She ran down the hill and lost the ring. I thought I would die. In tears, I told my mother about the lost ring, and she did nothing, nor did my aunt. No one paid attention to my sadness about my loss. Would anyone ever console me, who felt so alone and unheard? My cousin got away with losing my ring. I had a plan. My aunt had a ring in her dresser drawer and I planned to steal it to replace my lost ring. I went into the bedroom and found the ring and slipped it on my finger. My aunt caught me and called my mother down to her apartment and told her that I had stolen her ring. My mother came through the door like a hurricane, did not ask any questions, headed toward me, and immediately started to beat me and scream at me.

She screamed, "I did not teach you to be a thief. How could you do such a thing!"

I felt like a trapped mouse with no possibility of escape. After being slapped on the arms and back several times, I collapsed to the floor, and she started kicking me in my thighs until they were black and blue. I thought I was going to die. No one came to my rescue. Even the neighbors, who heard the noise and my crying, did not respond. My two cousins were standing there, watching and laughing.

They said, "You got punished, ha, ha."

My aunt stood there as if she were watching a bull being killed in the arena while applauding the matador. I was so hurt and humiliated. Crouched in a corner like a wounded animal licking its wounds and with no one to comfort me, I wanted to die. After a while, I got up and ran to my father's candy store. He hugged me and made me malted milk to make me feel better. I did feel better, but my body still ached from the beating. Years later, when I mentioned the beating to my mother, she did not remember it at all. She was embarrassed and humiliated in front of her sister by my action, so she probably buried the incident within her. Now I realize that I humiliated my mother in front of her younger sister and my two cousins. After all, my mother was the older sister and she and her children should be perfect. What an impossible message to have going on in your head and then to carry out. It took me a long time to come to this realization, but I finally have inner peace about it instead of harboring anger toward my mother regarding the incident. I have moved forward and that is so freeing.

Many years later in life, my mother admitted that as the oldest of three girls she was the one who was punished the most and had the most responsibility. One day, she fell asleep instead of completing her chores, so she was beaten by her father.

She learned to parent as she had been parented. When she told me how strictly she had been disciplined, I could better understand that strictness transferring into her. As an adult, I was able to let go of my anger and write a loving eulogy to her.

Finally, in second grade, my cousins moved away, and I was glad but a part of me did miss them. I made other friends, and I looked forward to school. I had perfect attendance throughout grade school because that way I could see my friends. Although my mother was a strict disciplinarian and I thought she was just plain mean, she did buy me nice clothes. Buying me things was her way of showing me love, but what I needed was to be supported and heard. She bought me a beautiful yellow dress, which I wore as proudly as a queen. She always ironed my clothes better than a commercial laundry. Teachers and friends often remarked that I had the best ironed clothes. I was proud of my mother's ironing skills, which I have never developed. I avoid ironing at all costs. On my twelfth birthday, my mother took me to my favorite store, Darlings, which was a doll store located on Third Avenue in the South Bronx. She purchased a beautiful doll for me with a pink dress and hat. The doll had blonde hair and blue eyes and looked like my sister Betty who was born in 1950 right after my ninth birthday. Oh, how I loved that doll. My mother even crocheted an additional pink bonnet for her. I took the doll on every trip I made. When I moved to Denver, Colorado, for my first job, the doll came with me. I enjoyed her and looked at her on my bed for the three years I lived in Denver. After three years, I decided to move back to New York. I asked my roommates to take the doll with them to New York because they left before me. Once in New York, I asked for my doll, and they said that they did not have her. She had disappeared. I cried and cried because I felt that I had lost a positive connection to my mother.

What was I to do with my despair? I started collecting dolls wherever I went. I bought dolls in Jamaica, Japan, Korea, Thailand, Germany, Slovakia, Greece, Iceland, England, and Spain. I had so many dolls but no place for them. I asked a friend to build me a doll house. He built one the size of a one-car garage. He also lined the walls with shelves for the dolls. Finally, the dolls had a home of their own. It is as big as a doll museum. At the entrance hangs a picture of my sister and me with the lost doll. All the dolls in the doll house are siblings to the lost doll. Under the window are many bride dolls and one groom doll. All these bride dolls are competing for the one groom. Which one will win? I would put my bet on the redhead because I love red hair. I even have a Princess Diana bride doll and Sarah Ferguson as a bride. Both wore exquisite dresses. One cubicle has dolls from Japan, Korea, and Thailand. The Asian dolls have bright-colored outfits and all look so elegant. I don't remember the Japanese and Korean women wearing such bright colors and elegant outfits. The Asian dolls must be the exception and not the norm. Another cubicle contains Native American dolls from different tribes. The simple outfits ornamented with beads and jewelry are so attractive to observe. A third cubicle contains dolls from Slovakia. The Slovak dolls are my favorites because they were made by my cousins. They are dressed in the Slovak kroj, reminding me of the clothes my aunts and cousins wore. They dressed me in the kroj when I visited Slovakia, and I looked like a real Slovak woman. The women have their heads covered with a cotton scarf and on Sundays they wear a lace headdress. I have a pink cotton scarf headpiece that they made for me when I visited. I still wear it to costume parties. Slovak costumes are colorful, and I like bright colors. The Slovaks are skilled in handicrafts, so the women do knitting, crocheting, and needlepoint and the men are skilled in woodworking. Most of the Slovak dolls are handmade, exhibiting the Slovak skills. In the next cubicle are dolls from Germany, where I lived and worked for eighteen years. The German dolls are wearing colorful outfits and I often saw the German women at festivals or dances wearing the traditional outfits. They did not wear the German outfits in everyday life, but in Slovakia the outfits that the dolls have on were worn by the women. In addition, there are dolls from Iceland, Alaska, and Greece. My Icelandic doll wears a black dress with a white headpiece. The outfit is beautiful in its simplicity. The Greek doll wears a colorful outfit with gold jewelry. Whenever I lived or traveled somewhere, I would look for a doll to take the place of the lost doll. I have dolls representing the characters in the novel *Gone with the Wind*. There is Scarlett O'Hara, Rhett Butler, and Mammy. They are part of the Tara plantation in Clayton County, Georgia. The ladies' long dresses were pretty, but I am not sure how comfortable they were. I prefer comfort over beauty! I typically wear a skirt with a comfortable matching top. At times, I will wear dress slacks and a loose-fitting top. I don't wear tight-fitting clothes. There are a few fairy tale dolls, including Red Riding Hood, Snow White, and Rapunzel. There are Disney characters such Mickey Mouse and Minnie Mouse. Finally, there are American dolls from different eras of American society. Anyone who has the privilege to enter the doll house becomes wide-eyed and amazed at the enormous collection of dolls in one house. Many friends suggested that I do something with all the dolls. I spoke to Marlene Hochman, who is president of the Toy Museum of New York, and she and I made an educational project of the doll collection. Noah Scofield made a video of all the dolls in the doll house. We placed the video on the museum's website so many people can access it and think about their own collections. Now the doll house with all its dolls has a purpose. My mother would have loved my doll collection because she was a collector. My mother's stuffed dog, whom she named Hector, has a place in my doll house. He watches over and protects the dolls from harm. We bought Hector in Germany at a vendor fair on the base. My mother loved Hector because he reminded her of a dog she had in Slovakia. She kept him by her bed and would wish him good night when she went to sleep.

EARLY LIFE IN AMERICA

I wanted to better understand my relationship with Mama, so I asked her many questions about her life, starting with her birth. Anna Jozefek was born on June 15, 1917, in Muskegon Heights, Michigan. Historically, Muskegon was inhabited by various bands of the Ottawa and Potawatomi tribes. The name Muskegon is derived from the Ottawa tribe, meaning "marshy river or swamp." It has a port on Lake Michigan. My maternal grandfather went to Muskegon Heights because his older brother John was already there. There were lots of opportunities for work, so my grandfather ventured out for better economic opportunities. He and my grandmother settled in a nice house near the center of town, which is where my mother was born. Muskegon Heights was a working-class area and my grandfather worked at Enterprise Brass Works, as did his brother John. I did not know that my grandfather worked at a brass factory until recently, when my cousin Pearl told me that her grandfather worked at a brass factory. Her grandfather was my grandfather's older brother John. My mother never mentioned what my grandfather did in Michigan. So, I learned a piece of history. The factory was in Muskegon Heights at the corner of Sanford and Manahan Streets. They specialized in pumps and valve systems. Brass is an alloy made of copper and zinc and is non-ferrous. It is known for its high conductivity, a relatively low melting point, and its resistance to corrosion. It is very malleable, formed into shapes and extruded without losing its strength and more malleable than bronze or zinc. It was encouraging to learn that my grandfather held a job that produced brass pumps and valves that were of value to society in the early 1900s. Unfortunately, the factory no longer exists. Kirk Bunke of Lakeshore Museum sent me information and a picture of the brass factory. It was so exciting to receive this information regarding my family history on my mother's side because I did not know that my grandfather worked in a brass factory. He went from being a farmer to being a brass factory worker. That was quite a change in occupations. He made an honest living at the brass factory to provide for a wife and a daughter. Soon, a second daughter joined the family. Anna's sister Susie was born fifteen months after her. My grandmother had two young girls to take care of, and they were a handful. Anna was obedient, but Susie was the rebellious one. They both liked Michigan and they would run around in their backyard. Life was good.

But when Anna was five, her world changed. Her parents decided to return to Vrbovce, Slovakia, their homeland. I will never understand why my maternal grandparents decided to return to Slovakia. Was the yearning for the homeland so great? Did they not realize how the move would affect their two American-born daughters? Anna cried because she would miss her friends and the trees and flowers of Michigan. In her book *The Abandoned Child Within*, Dr. Kathrin Asper writes, "A change of residence can evoke a sense of rootlessness." Such a person does not know where she belongs. I think I have remained in my present house for over twenty years because it gives me a sense of being rooted. Anna seemed to have one foot in Slovakia and the other in Michigan. She felt that she never belonged, and this permeated throughout her entire life. Perhaps if she had remained in Michigan, she would have had a sense of home and belonging. In addition, she would have been in the state of her birth. She always told people that she was born in Michigan, as if that was her identity. Muskegon Heights is on the water and

Slovakia is landlocked. I think that living near water if one is drawn to the water is a must. I wonder if my mother missed living near the water of Michigan. What else did she miss about Michigan? I will never know. She could not rebel nor remain in Michigan with a friend because her parents ruled. "Emotional abandonment of the child creates uncertainty about her feelings—whether she ought to be having them, and even what they are," writes Dr. Kathrin Asper. She also notes, "Not being well grounded in her own feeling life, such an individual tends to be top heavy, centered in her head, and to conform excessively to collective value. Emotional abandonment leaves one scarred into adulthood and even unto death unless one has the opportunity for therapy." I always felt guilty about any feelings I had, and I did not share my feelings with anyone. I bottled them up and suffered from anxiety throughout my early years. After a colleague encouraged me to seek therapy, I started to heal very slowly.

Anna had to say goodbye to Michigan and move to a foreign land—a land that had no real identity until 1993, when Slovakia became an independent republic. When Anna was transported to a foreign country in the early 1900s, the area was known as Czechoslovakia. Czechoslovakia was formed as an independent country in 1918 after World War I and was made up of three main groups: Czechs, Slovaks, and Moravians. All three groups were considered Slavic, but they had different languages and customs.

Prior to the formation of Czechoslovakia, the Slovaks were part of the Austro-Hungarian Empire. My grandfather's birth certificate states that he was born in Hungary, and he had to study Hungarian at school. The Slovak language and customs were considered secondary under the Austro-Hungarian Empire, so the Slovak people were without their identity. Even in Czechoslovakia, many Slovaks felt that the country was dominated by the Czechs, and they felt like secondary citizens. So, being taken out of her land of birth to a country whose identity was submerged must have had a negative effect on the self-esteem of my mother. As an adult, she spoke of being removed from Michigan with sadness. Anna did not want to move away from Michigan, the land of her birth. She spoke English and had started school in Michigan, and now that was going to end. Oh, how Anna cried to leave her friends and the country of her birth to live in a foreign country. She begged to stay with friends, but she had no voice in the matter. She wondered how she would communicate in this foreign country. Would anyone speak English? So many questions went through her mind.

MOVE TO
CZECHOSLOVAKIA

The day of departure from Michigan was a sad day for Anna. They traveled by train to New York, where they boarded a boat. The trip took a long time. She wondered if she would ever see land again. She was even seasick. The boat landed in Bremerhaven, Germany, which was quite far from Czechoslovakia. They disembarked and walked about a mile to a train station. The train took them to Bratislava, a main city in the Slovak part of Czechoslovakia. At least the train was clean and fairly comfortable. They were all exhausted from the ten-hour train ride and still had to find a bus, which would take them to Vrbovce, which is near Myjava. The old and dirty-looking bus was not far from the train station, so they boarded the bus and rode for two hours before they arrived in Vrbovce. Once they got off the bus, they had to walk up a steep hill to reach their house. What a long and tedious trip they made from Michigan to Czechoslovakia. I am not sure I could have survived it. I applaud my mother for surviving and thriving. Once they reached the house, they wanted to just sleep. Fortunately, there were beds in the house and some food that the neighbors had provided. They had a nice house, which her father had purchased before he'd gone to America.

Now that Anna was in Vrbovce, she had anxiety about school, friends, and home. Would she relate to the other children in school? Would she be ostracized as an American? She wore American clothes and now she had to dress in the Slovak kroj (costume), which was uncomfortable. She didn't even know how to put on these strange garments. Oh, how she longed to return to America. She thought she could find a way back to Michigan. She thought maybe a teacher in school could help her find a way back to Michigan. That never happened. Yes, even in the twentieth century, the kroj was worn. When I visited Slovakia in 1995, my aunts and cousins were still wearing the kroj. They kept wearing the traditional garb until they died. They never made the transition to modern clothing.

A year later, Anna's youngest sister, Kristine, was born in Slovakia. As the youngest, she was spoiled. Anna and Susie had to do all the work and Kristine could play. How they both resented her. After Kristine was born, Anna's mother (my grandmother) decided to leave her three daughters with my grandfather and return to America. She went to New York City, where her mother, my great-grandmother, was living. So, my mother and her sisters were without a mother for many years. I could not understand how a mother could leave three young daughters and go to live in another place without them. This action was a puzzle to me all my life. My grandmother died at the age of forty-four, when I was only two years old. I never had the opportunity to ask her about her actions. I asked my mother about her departure, but she never gave me an answer. All she would say is that when her mother visited them three years later, they did not recognize her. She seemed a strange woman to her and her sisters. My mother felt that her mother did not like her. She was without a mother's love. How sad for her! No wonder she could not give her love to her daughters. Her paternal grandmother lived near Anna and her sisters in Vrbovce, but was not welcoming. Whenever they would visit, she would say, "Here come Martin's brats." So, my mother remembers being one of her father's brats. What does that do for a child's self-esteem? I can now better understand some of my mother's actions. As an adult, she frequently made friends with older women as if she were still looking for a mother connection. Here she was in Slovakia, and she had to make the best of it.

She did well in school, and she really liked art, though she never had the opportunity to develop her artistic talents. After completing her education at the local school, she was selected to attend a gymnasium in another town named Skalica. She was the only one in Vrbovce to be selected for further education. She was excited because she would live in a dorm and make new friends. Two of her good friends were Jewish. It was before Hitler invaded Czechoslovakia and there were many Jews living in Vrbovce and the neighboring small towns. Years later, when she heard that they had died in a concentration camp, she was sad and she cried. Their deaths made her feel like a part of her had died with them. However, her studies were going well, and she enjoyed her friends. She wanted to become a teacher and was now on her way to achieving her goal.

But suddenly, another change occurred in her life. Her father kept up with the news and knew that World War II was on the horizon. He decided to protect her and her sister Susie by sending them back to America to live with their estranged mother. He did not send Kristine, the youngest sister, because she was not born in America. After that point, the sisters were separated forever and lived very different lives. Kristine remained in the family house in Vrbovce for her entire life. My grandfather married her off at the age of fourteen to an older man so they could take care of the house. He then went to America to join my grandmother and his two American daughters. What a blow that was to Anna. Here she had settled in Slovakia and now she was going back to America. What would she do in America? She wasn't even going to Michigan, but instead to New York City to a mother she hardly knew. Her anxiety was so great. Again, she had no chance to discuss this with her father. He'd made the decision and he ruled. So, she reluctantly accepted that she was moving back to America.

I had the opportunity to visit Slovakia for the first time in 1973. My aunt told me that the German soldiers came and demanded food and drink. She said they were polite though demanding. She said when the Russians came after WWII and took over Czechoslovakia, they were brutal. They were demanding and when they did not give them food or their land, they were beaten. My uncle resisted the land takeover, so he was beaten brutally by the Russian soldiers. My cousin's husband remembered seeing the German soldiers taking the local Jewish people, shooting them, and then throwing them over the hill. He was frightened by what he'd observed as a young boy. There is a Jewish cemetery in Vrbovce, but it is overgrown and many of the stones have fallen down. Since WWII, there have been no Jewish inhabitants in Vrbovce. It was through Jewish agents that many of the people of Vrbovce were able to travel to America. They would pay the agent a certain amount of money and he would arrange the passage to America. In 1973, it was not very different from the early 1900s, when my mother was there. The women still wore the kroj, and there were very few cars there. The people walked to town and rode buses or trains to travel longer distances. The country was still called Czechoslovakia and the people resented the Czechs. It seemed as if the Slovak part of the country stood still in time. I visited the home where my mother spent several years of her life. It was a spacious home with many windows. The rooms didn't have much furniture, but they were clean and neat. The beds were always made. They had feather blankets on them to keep everyone warm. The local ladies made the feather beds using real goose feathers. I appreciated the rolling hills and the cherry trees. The linden tree with its heart-shaped leaves was my favorite. The tea from the flowers of the linden tree is delicious and so soothing. It would remedy a stomachache. The food was fresh and the homemade breads were mouthwatering. I could devour a whole loaf at a time. I enjoyed the pea and mushroom soups that my aunts made. I don't like sausage, but the homemade sausage was the best and the only one I will ever eat. Standing outside the house and looked at the land of my ancestors, I had a feeling of belonging. Here, nature was at its finest. The beauty of the land was soothing to my soul. The sunflowers stood erect, like soldiers in formation. The memories of Slovakia are imprinted on my brain like a beautiful photograph.

However, in 1973, Czechoslovakia was a communist country, and I had to obtain a visa to enter the country. I had to be careful what I said and aware of who might be watching me. I saw Russian soldiers wherever I went. My cousins had to study Russian in school and learn about Russian leaders. I remember both my uncle and grandfather telling me about and showing me the land they owned, which was taken over by the communists. They were left with only a small plot and the rest was gone to become part of the collective farm run by the Russians. At times, I was glad that my parents and I had been born in America, where I pursue my dreams more readily. For my mother, it must have been disappointing to leave beautiful Slovakia and come to New York City with its tall buildings and treeless areas. My mother must have been heartbroken to leave all that natural beauty. First, she had to leave Michigan; then, she had to leave Slovakia.

BACK TO AMERICA

My mother, Anna, was fourteen years old, and she had to leave Slovakia behind. Her sister Susie did not travel with her because my grandfather had to save some money to send her a year later. My mother was sad to leave her sisters behind, but was happy to see Susie a year later. There were a few other people traveling to America, so they would take care of her. She had to take several trains to Bremerhaven, Germany, where she would board a big ship that took her to New York. I cannot imagine traveling on a big ship at the age of fourteen. I would be crying all the way to America. It was a seven-day voyage. She was seasick for about three days, so she did not eat. She wondered if they would ever make it to land. She was tired of seeing just water. It was a boring trip because there were few young girls on the boat, and she knew only a few people who spoke Slovak. All the service people on the boat spoke German and she studied German in school so she could speak with them. After seven long days, she was finally glad to see land. In the darkness, she was amazed to see what appeared to be mountains and later realized were many tall buildings. In the dark, they appeared to be mountains. But once in America, her mother met her at the pier. They took a train to the apartment where her mother lived in lower Manhattan. It was a small apartment and was crowded. Now, she missed the open spaces and trees of Slovakia. New York City was too big for her. She didn't want to be there, but what was she to do? She wondered what other turns her life would take. Soon, her mother found her a job as a nanny for a Jewish family in the west Bronx. While she worked and lived with them, her sister Susie went to work with her mother in the evenings cleaning offices after the occupants left for the day. Anna missed seeing Susie on a daily basis, but her family would arrange for Susie to visit her once a month. They would eat a meal together with the family and talk about their times in Michigan and Czechoslovakia. Susie didn't like the family Anna worked for because she felt that they took advantage of Anna. She felt they gave her too much work to do. Susie preferred cleaning offices. Susie and Anna remained close until Susie died in her early seventies. Kristine, the youngest sister, was out of the picture because she remained in Czechoslovakia and they really didn't miss her too much.

The father of the family Anna nannied for was a dentist, and the wife was a stay-at-home mom with one son named Harold. My mother would clean for them and do dishes. She had her own room and plenty of kosher food to eat. She learned to make kosher food, and it was her favorite food throughout her life. She liked to eat lox on a bagel and so did I. She also liked matzah with a butter spread. Kosher foods fall into three categories: meat, dairy, and pareve. Fish and poultry are sometimes included in pareve. The Torah says kosher means food can only come from animals that have split hooves and chew their cud like cows, sheep, and goats. Foods that meet the kosher dietary laws are labeled with one of the kosher symbols including K, Circle U, and Circle K. You can usually find these symbols in small type on the bottom front of the package. Jews do not mix dairy and meat. The Torah forbids the cooking and consumption of any milk with any meat to prevent one from cooking a kind in its mother's milk. I was in the Catskill Mountains in New York with a college group of friends and at one of the meals I asked for milk. The waiter said that you do not drink milk with meat, so I had water instead. That was my introduction to a kosher rule. To this day I do not mix meat and milk.

Anna enjoyed the family, and they made her feel welcome. The lady of the house arranged for her to attend night classes in English, and she was able to obtain a high school diploma. She enjoyed celebrating the Jewish holidays with the family. Her favorite holiday was Hanukkah because she received eight gifts, one for each day of the celebration. Perhaps my mother liked gift giving and enjoyed receiving gifts. Hanukkah commemorates the rededication of the temple in Jerusalem after it was defiled by the Seleucids in 164 BCE. The themes of this holiday include liberation from oppression, religious freedom, divine miracles, and courage. Hanukkah is the eight-day festival of lights and Jews light the menorah each night.

Life was good. She had a bed to sleep in and plenty to eat. How long would this life last for her? Was this going to be a lifetime career? After several years, my grandmother became busy once again and arranged for my mother to meet my father, John Plesa. They dated and married when she was nineteen years old, and my father was twenty-nine years old. Her Jewish family showered her with gifts and even attended her wedding. She was glad they were there because they had become her real family. Her mother and grandmother attended the wedding, but her father was absent because he was still in Slovakia. Her life of nineteen years had been one of movement and adjustment. I could not have coped with all those changes. My mother wanted to be a professional woman but instead succumbed to the collective and culture to marry and have children. She never took her own journey, but seemed to appease others around her. How sad to not be able to fulfill her goals in life. She gave up her dream of becoming a teacher and her interest in art in order to become a housekeeper, wife, and mother. As her daughter, perhaps it was my journey to become a professional woman, which I have done. As a child, I dreamed of going to college and being an educated woman.

I wanted to be a woman who would contribute to society in some way. I have had the opportunity to obtain a bachelor's degree in history, two master's degrees, and a doctorate in education. I had the opportunity to be a teacher and a therapist. How different from my mother's life.

MARRIAGE AND FAMILY

My mother /Anna said goodbye to her adopted family and she and my father rented an apartment on Pearl Street in lower Manhattan. My grandmother lived next door. My grandfather had married my Aunt Kristine off at the age of fourteen to a man twelve years her senior. My grandfather left her and her husband in the family home and went to America before World War II started. Since Aunt Kristine was not born in America, he left her in Czechoslovakia, where she was born. She had a husband to take care of her. I often wonder if he thought about how the splitting up of the sisters would affect them. I guess he did not see it from that perspective. He joined my grandmother in the apartment next door to my parents. My father worked as a busboy in a restaurant and my mother became a cleaning lady in commercial buildings in Manhattan. So, her dreams of becoming a teacher were crushed. How sad for her!

John and Anna were married for five years when, on October 8, 1941, Anna gave birth to a baby girl, whom she named Zuzana. I was born two months before Pearl Harbor, so I became known as a Pearl Harbor Baby. Grandmother was a big help to Anna with the baby and the baby connected with her. Whenever I went out with Grandmother, I always returned with a new bonnet or dress. Those first two and a half years with Mama and Grandmother were so happy for the little girl. However, Grandmother got sick with throat cancer (although she was not a smoker) and died at the age of forty-four, when I was only two and a half years old. According to my mother, she was in great pain, and in the early 1940s, there was not much relief from pain. Both my mother and her sister Susie took care of my grandmother until her death. As I got older, I did not remember my grandmother, to Anna's disappointment. I only remembered what I had been told.

I was told that she liked to take me to the park and shopping. Since I was a quiet and well-behaved child, my grandmother favored me. I apparently liked all the attention she gave me. She was buried in Brooklyn, New York, in a family plot at a cemetery named Linden Hill. I often visited her grave with my mother, and we planted flowers there. After Grandmother died, the family moved to Belcamp, Maryland, in 1942, where my father obtained a job at the Bata Shoe Factory. He worked on an assembly line in the process of making a shoe. I guess he enjoyed his job because he spoke about his days at Bata. He had a lot of friends, and he enjoyed the community.

Bata was founded in 1894 in Zlín, Austria-Hungary, which is now the Czech Republic. Tomas Bata, the founder, was a ninth-generation shoemaker in his family. The Czech owners came to the United States in 1932 because Hitler came to power in Germany. They feared that it would not bode well for European companies. They selected Belcamp, Maryland, as the site for their shoe company. They liked the area's central location in the Middle Atlantic region. They purchased 2,000 acres of land on the shore of the Bush River that included a historic farm. They built a five-story factory for the manufacture of shoes, a hotel, and seventy houses for the employees. It was a nice, self-contained community. My mother told me that I enjoyed playing with the other children in the nearby park area. My mother and I traveled to Maryland by train. Since it was still wartime, there were many soldiers on the train, and they gave me a lot of attention. My blue eyes sparkled as the soldiers talked to me. Anna was not happy in

Maryland, so in six months, we moved back to New York. I wish we had remained in Maryland because, from what I have read about Belcamp, it seemed like a pleasant and safe community. My sister once remarked that she wished that she had been born in Maryland instead of the Bronx. I guess Maryland has a more pleasant ring to it. Anna was never happy in any place we lived. She found something wrong with every house we lived in. I am not sure why. Perhaps she missed Michigan and Czechoslovakia. I think that she never fulfilled her goals, and she blamed the place instead of looking inside herself. I think she was unhappy after returning to America as a teenager.

My parents found an apartment in the south Bronx, where they lived for eleven years. It was on the third floor, and they had two bedrooms. Soon, my widowed grandfather moved in with them and occupied one of the bedrooms. I had no room of my own. I slept on a folding bed in the living room. It was opened at night and folded up in the morning. The apartment was crowded but they made it work. Sam's Delicatessen was next door to the apartment, as was Tommy's Candy Store. Those were the family's favorite places. Anna worked at cleaning jobs in the evenings and would catch up on sleep during the day. Her husband worked at restaurants both as a cook and waiter.

In 1950, a second daughter was born, and Anna and John named her Elizabeth, but she was called Betty. I was nine years old when Betty was born, but I was overjoyed to finally have a sister. I was tired of being an only child. I did have a lot of responsibility for the new baby, which I enjoyed, but I refused to change her diapers. Anna depended on me for paperwork and other activities. She felt like an immigrant instead of a natural-born American citizen. It seems that immigrant mothers depend on their children for many adult responsibilities. The firstborn is usually the one to take the parental role and feels that their childhood was taken away from them. Many children of immigrants have shared with me that they resent their mothers for all the responsibility they were given. In addition, the mothers wanted them to fit in, so they were criticized and punished if they did not live up to their mothers' standards. In many ways, mothers lived through their children. Anna wanted me to be the perfect child. In her eyes, children should be seen and not heard. If I did something wrong, she did not spare the rod. I was slapped or beaten many times without always understanding what I did wrong. Parenting seems to be generational. We learn by observing what our parents do. Anna was beaten by her father if she did not complete a task, so she parented in a similar manner. She remembered being beaten by her father because she had fallen asleep before she completed her chores. Anna and John both continued to work full-time, while I attended the local public schools.

Betty was taken care of by each parent when not working outside the home. Anna's sister Susie moved to a farm in upstate New York to a town called East Berne. Susie had a son and daughter who were my age. She agreed to take Betty and care for her on the farm, so Betty spent her first few years with Aunt Susie. I was sad to have my sister taken away from me and cried about it but I did not have any say in the matter. I did visit the farm during summer vacation and that was the time I could spend with my sister. Finally, Anna and John had saved some money, so they decided to buy their own house and give up renting an apartment. They looked for houses that they could afford and finally found a two-family home in the north Bronx in the Pelham Bay Area. It was a beautiful home with three bedrooms. One for Anna and John, one for Grandfather, and one for me and Betty. I finally had a bed that I did not have to fold up each day. That was a step up. But I never had my own room until I graduated from college and started working as a teacher in Denver, Colorado.

I spent my high school years in the new house. I enjoyed the new neighborhood and made new friends. I did well in high school and appreciated the academic background I received at

Walton High School in the Bronx. During high school, I visited Wagner College in Staten Island and decided that I wanted to attend college there. So, after high school graduation at Carnegie Hall, I headed to Wagner College. I was excited because I would live in the dormitory and around other students. I entered as an elementary school major, but my roommate stated that this was not the right major for me. I listened to her because no one in my family attended college, so this was new territory for me. I thought everyone else knew more than me and especially about what I should study. I then changed my major to history and decided to become a high school teacher. In retrospect, history was not the right major for me. I would have rather majored in English or psychology. I really enjoy reading and writing, so English would have been ideal for me. I am now a Jungian Analyst and starting in the area of psychology would have been where I belonged. I did get into the profession that I enjoy, but it was later in life. College had its ups and downs. I didn't even know how to select a college. Sometimes I could concentrate on my studies, and at other times my mind was filled with anxiety. I worried about my parents and their relationship, as they seemed to be growing apart. My mother was depressed most of the time. I realized how much she depended on me for her joy in life. She seemed so lost in life with no real goals. I worked in an office during the summers and saved my money for the school year. My mother seemed happy when I was home for the summers. She cried whenever I returned to school, which made me feel guilty.

I saw pictures of Colorado and was drawn to the mountains. It seemed like such a beautiful place, so I made up my mind that I would move there after college graduation. It was meant to be because in the office where I had worked for five years, the Denver Public Schools had an account. The CEO made contact with the treasurer of the Denver Public Schools, and I was hired as a social studies teacher. My world seemed to be opening. My mother was devastated that I was moving so far away. When she visited me in Denver, she wanted to stay. I was in no position to take her on, so she returned to New York disappointed. I think she had abandonment issues and other psychological problems. At that time, I had no training in mental health, so I knew I could not handle her. She could not take any criticism and if I made a comment that she could not receive, she would stop speaking to me. I had to be away from her physically for my own mental health. It took me many years of personal counseling to develop self-care and move on from a negative relationship with my mother. I remained in Denver for three years and became restless. The mountains and scenery were no longer enough for me. I am not sure what I yearned for in particular, but I knew that something was missing for me. I moved to so many different places and thought that a new place would provide what my soul needed.

Through my Jungian studies, I finally came to the realization that we have to look inside ourselves and become aware of our needs, both physical and emotional. Yes, a sense of place is important, but moving from place to place is not the solution to our restlessness. I finally found my place of peace in Niceville, Florida, and have lived here since 1998. I chose this place because it is near Eglin Air Force Base and after working for the military overseas for thirty years, I wanted to transition back to the United States near a military base. This move was chosen carefully with divine inspiration and direction. My roommate was also a teacher and she talked me into applying to overseas schools. She had learned about the program in high school, but I'd never heard of it. She obtained a job in Frankfurt, Germany, and I was told to study another subject area in order to qualify for high school teaching. I was told by the recruiter that there was an overabundance of social studies teachers and without a second subject I could not compete. In addition, they wanted male coaches. As a female with only a social studies teaching background, I was not very competitive. I decided to move back to New York and get an English minor. I also wanted to get a master's degree from Hofstra University. I chose Hofstra because it was an easy drive from the Bronx, and I liked the campus. My mother was delighted that I was returning to New York. My father had sold the beautiful house and purchased an older home in another neighborhood. I obtained a teaching job in a New York City junior high school and went to school at night. I enjoyed my studies at Hofstra, and I made a few friends there. I even took several English classes that gave me the English minor I needed for a second teaching area. We would discuss teaching techniques during our breaks and before and after class. There were other teachers in the master's program, and in 1967, I obtained a master's degree in secondary education. I was proud of my accomplishment, but living with my family was too difficult. My father was drinking excessively, and my mother would then have her shouting outbursts. I needed a calm environment so I could concentrate on my studies. I found a basement apartment a few miles away from my parents. It was not a very attractive place, but at least I had peace and quiet. One of my teacher friends helped me move to the new apartment. I had several good friends who taught with me at Sousa Junior High School. I taught social studies and English after I had enough English courses. The teachers and I would go to plays and dinners together. Socially, I had a great life. The job of teaching in New York City was very difficult and tiring. I was drained at the end of each day. The discipline problems were so difficult. The job was so different from the one in Denver. I even wondered why I ever left Denver. I had no classroom of my own and had to travel to a different room for each class. Moving around meant that I had to carry materials from place to place. I felt that I was set up for failure. There was very little administrative support because they were inundated with paperwork and parent conferences. I could not continue working in this environment and I admired the teachers who did it for many years. I was a professional woman and I wanted to experience some job satisfaction, but I could not in New York City. Meanwhile, on the home front, my mother would visit me often and complain about my father. I couldn't help her, but I felt badly for her. She was depressed and crying all the time.

After three years in New York City, I decided to reapply to the overseas schools. This time I was accepted, and my first assignment was to Guantanamo Bay, Cuba. I was delighted but my mother was upset because I would not be there for her. I realized how much she leaned on me. It was as if I was the mother and she the child. Guantanamo Bay, Cuba, was like paradise both physically and job-wise. I did well with the warm weather, and I loved going to the beach. Swimming in the blue waters was such a relaxing experience. The sunsets were the most beautiful in the world. Since there were many ships that came to Guantanamo, the teachers were allowed to go with them on weekend trips. All we had to do was sign up. We would leave on Friday and return on Monday morning just in time for work. I had the opportunity to go to Jamaica twice, Haiti once, and Puerto Rico once. Jamaica had beautiful beaches, good food, and friendly people. The dancing at Jamaica clubs was fun and good exercise. They also spoke English in Jamaica. Haiti was so different from Jamaica because there was a dictatorship, so the people did not feel free to be friendly. There was so much poverty there and the children were always following us and begging. French was the main language and I studied French in school, but I did not speak with many people. I never returned to Haiti. Puerto Rico was beautiful, and the people were friendly. I enjoyed the beautiful beaches and the National Forest in San Juan. Besides the benefits of travel and the beauty of Guantanamo Bay, the teaching job was so rewarding. The students were disciplined and eager to learn. I had my own classroom and we had ample books and supplies. The parents appreciated the teachers, and the administration was supportive. What a difference from teaching in

New York City! I considered this my dream job because I was appreciated and treated like a professional. The teachers were friendly, and we had dinners and parties together. I loved the warm climate and did not miss the snow of New York City. Our living quarters consisted of one room with shared bathrooms and kitchens. We did not have to pay for our living quarters, so that was a good feature. We could save a lot of money because there was not much to buy. Since it was warm, we didn't need sweaters, coats, or boots. The clothing we wore was not expensive. I felt very fortunate to be in Guantanamo Bay for one year. One day toward the end of the year, the principal came into my classroom to inform me that I had received a transfer to Misawa, Japan. I jumped for joy, and I thanked the principal for bringing me the good news.

I had always wanted to go to Japan because I had a Japanese pen pal in high school. I met him while in Japan and he showed me around Tokyo. He was a policeman, and he knew the city well. What a treat to have a private tour guide in Tokyo. My mother had to find other people to help her survive because I was leaving her and going to the other end of the world. She did find a few friends who would mother her. After four years overseas, I quit and went to California to attend Fuller Seminary. I obtained a degree in marriage and family counseling. This degree came about quite by default. I was going to Fuller Seminary upon the recommendation of a Navy chaplain because I wanted to develop the spiritual side of myself. I had been in a Bible study group in Japan, and I wanted to further my biblical studies, so to Fuller Seminary I went.

Upon arrival at the seminary, I was without direction. I didn't know what courses to take nor what major to select. The registrar suggested I talk with Dr. Bowers, who was in charge of the marriage and family counseling program. I met with him, and he set up a program of studies for me with a degree in marriage and family counseling. I was registered in a marriage and family practicum, which was in North

Hollywood, where I met many new students. There were a few of us from Fuller Seminary and those people became my friends during my three years at Fuller. So, here I was again, in a program that someone else had suggested. I believed in family and wanted something better than my family of origin. I thought I would make the best of the situation. I went from elementary education to a history major, then to an English minor and now marriage counseling. So many changes in my life and all at the suggestion of someone else. Where was my core in all this? I allowed everyone else to dictate my journey. I met another student named Scott who became my friend for the three years that I was at Fuller. He suggested that I become a Jungian Analyst and that I study at the Jung Institute in Zurich, Switzerland. I said I would give the idea some thought. That idea became reality several years later. In reflection on the direction of my life in relation to my mother, I became aware that I gave my decision-making power to others. It is as if I buried my own thoughts and ideas because I did not value myself. I also realized that this was my mother's pattern and here I was following in her footsteps. My sister and mother attended my graduation. It was good to see them there but I was glad when my mother left. I spent three years in California, and they were fruitful years. But my mother was so negative the whole time she was in California.

After graduation, I needed a full-time job because my savings were depleted, and the part-time jobs could not keep me above water financially. I was offered a teaching position at a local high school, but the salary was not enough to sustain even my simple lifestyle in California. I decided not to remain in California and reapplied to overseas schools. I knew that the overseas school would provide housing and a better salary. There also was a good federal retirement system. In addition, there were opportunities to teach in different countries around the world. All this was much more appealing than remaining in California. Soon, I received a letter that I was accepted and was offered a position in Wurzburg, Germany. I was so excited about going to Germany that I told one of my friends I was going to paradise.

Paradise turned out to be a place of difficult adjustment. There was no housing on base, so I had to find an apartment in the German economy. I lived in a hotel on base for a month before a teacher at the high school found me a basement apartment. It was a cold apartment and very small. The German landlords lived upstairs, and I felt as if I was under scrutiny the whole time. They had access to my apartment at all times and this was difficult for the private person that I am. How different from my lovely California apartment that was spacious and private. I missed the apartment pool that I had in California. Paradise was looking dim. Then there was the written driving test that I had to take. I had to take it twice because I could not concentrate on it the first time. I did succeed the second time. I had to buy a car because I had sold the Honda I had in California. I bought a used Volkswagen and that worked well. All of these transitions were difficult for me while trying to teach five classes each day. After a year, I was able to adjust to German living. I met a German friend who lived near me and she and I would walk each morning before work. That was the highlight of my day. Inge and I took short trips, and we would eat in German restaurants. I took a German language course at the university and did quite well in learning to speak German. I made several new German friends and I still keep in touch with Inge.

I also made a lifelong friend, Ralph, who was an industrial arts teacher at Wurzburg High School. We had many professional discussions as educators. We lost contact for several years while I was in England and Iceland. Since his retirement and move back to the States, we have been in contact. We have even taken a few trips to South Florida, Georgia, and Alabama. We were good travel companions. Since he has developed some medical problems, we have not been able to do much together. Our contact was by telephone, and he was a good listener. I enjoyed talking with him. Suddenly, on the morning of March 6, 2024, I received a telephone call from Ralph's sister that he had passed away. I was devastated. My good friend and listener had died. I cried so much that I did not have any more tears left. I did a few things to help me with the grieving process. I asked my pastor to pray for him and I had flowers put on the altar of my church in his memory. In addition, I asked the overseas schools organization (AOSHS) to place a virtual remembrance on their website. Those actions brought some relief to me. I also notified some of my friends regarding his death and their support was so welcomed. Developing friendships in Wurzburg made me enjoy the place and I ended up staying in there for eight years.

My mother visited me twice in Wurzburg and we drove to Slovakia. She seemed to enjoy our visits to Slovakia because my cousins gave her a lot of attention and love. We visited the schools she attended, and we also visited one of her school friends. She could relive some of the happy moments in her early years in Slovakia.

In 1979, another change occurred in her life. My father fell down the stairs in the house and died. My mother was now a widow living alone in the house. She had difficulty living alone particularly because she was not handy with fixing things such as a leaky faucet. House maintenance was my father's responsibility. She had to depend on others to fix things and sometimes they overcharged her. She attended the Senior Citizens Center and barely survived for eight years. I left Wurzburg after eight years to go on educational leave for one year. I went to Winter Park, Florida, where I bought a small house and attended courses at the University of Central Florida. I made many friends and enjoyed my courses. I did substitute teaching at the local schools. I attended St. John's Lutheran Church and really felt part of that community. At the end of my leave year, I was reassigned to Stuttgart, Germany, as the director of a special education program.

One Sunday in Stuttgart, while I was relaxing in my apartment, the phone rang and it was my sister. I knew it meant trouble because my sister rarely called me. She said that my mother had sold her house in the Bronx and the closing was in two weeks. She had no plan as to where she would go. What to do! I was at my wit's end. She was telling everyone that she was going to live in the senior citizen building, but she had not even put in an application. My sister said that she could not take her because she had enough to do with two teenagers and a spouse. I stated that I could not come to the closing in two weeks. My sister said that she would postpone the closing until July, when I could come to the house sale in New York City. The next question was where to put my mother once the house had been sold. I tried different housing possibilities in New York City, but the waiting lists were miles long. I prayed and prayed and finally decided to have her come to Germany and live with me. I prepared a room for her, and my sister was to put her on the plane. That was the plan. I met her in Stuttgart and the next six years of my life were a test of endurance.

LIFE IN STUTTGART, GERMANY

Living with my mother would not be easy because I had to work all day at a high school, but I had two bedrooms and I prepared one for her. I flew to New York, and both my sister and I attended the closing of the sale of my mother's house. I bought my mother a ticket; she was to fly two weeks after I returned to Germany. She could stay in the house for two more weeks. My sister and I had cleaned out most of the house before the closing. She and my friend, Ann, were to take my mother to the airport in New York, and I would meet her at the airport in Stuttgart. I needed the time to prepare the apartment for my mother, so I flew to Germany two weeks before her.

The day of my mother's arrival came very quickly, and my neighbor Peter volunteered to go to the airport with me. Stuttgart airport was not very big, so I did not anticipate any problems. How wrong I was. After the plane arrived and all the passengers had departed, my mother was nowhere to be found. Oh, where was she? I wondered if she had gotten off the plane in another city. I waited by the gate and Peter went looking for her. He did not know what she looked like, but he came back and said he saw a short, dark-haired lady on the other side. I went with him and that was my mother. She had wandered off in the wrong direction. She was tired and confused, but she smiled when she saw me coming toward her. Now that I had found her, we went to my car and drove to my apartment. I lived on the third floor of an elevated building. There was a big balcony and she liked that because she could see a view of the city. I showed her the bedroom that I had prepared for her, and she was happy to be with me. I made her a ham and cheese sandwich on some fresh German bread and some coffee. I had to go to work on Monday and she had to stay in the apartment all by herself.

I found an agency that sends people to help the elderly. A young German girl would come and draw pictures with my mother. Another young man named George came too; he was from the Czech Republic and was working in Germany. The Czech and Slovak languages are similar, so he and my mother could speak in Slovak. Although George grew up in Prague, his father was Slovak, so he could speak and understand both languages. He became a family friend and was helpful to us throughout my stay in Germany. He would take my mother for walks and to the local stores, which she enjoyed. She had difficulty walking because she had a bad knee. She was in pain most of the time. One of the doctors on the American base in Stuttgart gave her a wheelchair so that George could take her on longer trips. The doctor at the American hospital on base x-rayed her knee and said she needed surgery. He said that they did not do the surgery in Germany. He recommended that she go through the German system instead of going to the States for the surgery. She eventually had knee surgery in a German hospital. The surgeon had an excellent reputation and was referred by a German orthopedic doctor that my mother saw prior to the surgery. George went with us to the hospital and was very helpful. His German was better than mine, so he translated anything that I did not understand. The surgery went well, and a few weeks later, my mother attended water therapy on a weekly basis. She could walk again without pain. In addition, my mother needed special shoes for walking, so the orthopedic doctor gave her a prescription. We went to the shoe cobbler, and he made her two pairs of shoes. One pair was beige, and the other pair was black. She could walk better in her new shoes, and she even enjoyed walking outside. She felt like she had new feet. We would take walks in the neighborhood and admire the flowers the Germans had planted. The red geraniums were our favorites and we planted some in window boxes on our balcony. I wish I could find a shoe cobbler in America who would make shoes to fit my feet.

My mother liked to draw and liked art, but she had forgotten how to draw. Together, we bought some coloring books and crayons. She could fill in the blanks and that would occupy her time during the day when I was working. When I came home from work, she was excited to show me what she colored. It was art therapy for her. When she completed several coloring books, we drove to the bookbinder with them. He was an older gentleman, and he provided a chair for my mother while we picked out the binding. He bound all her coloring books. She felt as if she was a published artist. Art therapy lifted her spirits and was good medicine for her self-esteem.

I was grateful for the help George and Sabrina provided for my mother. She was thriving in Germany and doing well. She liked the apartment we lived in. My neighbor, Peter, was kind and helpful. He would share meals with us. He was a good cook, and his German potato salad was the best in the world. But then suddenly, we received a notice that the owner of the apartment was selling it and we had to move. Oh, what a disruption for both of us! Finding a new apartment was difficult and time-consuming. Two-bedroom apartments were in demand, so one had to wait a long time to find one. In addition, the apartments were expensive. The process of allowing strange people to come and look at our apartment was so frustrating. I thought I was providing a stable home for my mother and here we were, encountering another move.

One of my colleagues found us an apartment in another part of Stuttgart. This apartment had bigger bedrooms and a newer kitchen, and there was an American teacher in the building who invited us to dinner. Another colleague lived in the next building, and we socialized with him and his spouse. We packed our belongings, and some friends helped us move. George no longer worked for the organization that provided help, but he remained a friend and visited us in the new apartment. Sabrina no longer visited my mother because the new apartment was too far away from her home. I had to find new help for my mother. The new apartment was on the fifth floor with a pleasant balcony view. Fortunately, the family across the hall was from the Czech Republic and the wife checked in on my mother daily. That was such a relief and blessing. We celebrated holidays with this family and their daughter, Sharon, became like family. We enjoyed this apartment and our neighbors. My mother was happy, and she spent her days watering our flowers and knitting.

On my fiftieth birthday, my mother gave me two rings. One was a gold ring with her initials, AJ, on two hearts. The gold ring was one my mother had been given as a young girl by her parents at her confirmation. I appreciated that it was passed on to me as a family inheritance. The other was my grandmother's garnet ring that was bought in Prague. The name "garnet" derives from the Latin word for grain due to the similarity between their rounded crystals. Garnet signifies protection, friendship, trust, commitment, and love. Garnet is also said to keep the wearer safe during travel, and that it did for me. I like the redness of the garnet because red is a color of energy. Both rings were a connection to my mother and grandmother and to the feminine line in our family. It took me a long time to realize that the rings were a gesture of love and acceptance. She was a gift giver. Again, I realized that the doll she had given me for my twelfth birthday, and I later lost, was my mother's way of showing love. We continued to celebrate holidays and birthdays in Stuttgart, Germany. My mother's seventy-fifth birthday was celebrated with a cake, ice cream, and coffee. Several friends were invited to celebrate her birthday. It was a happy day for us, but our happiness was about to end because our second apartment was being sold and we had to move again. This would be a third move for my mother and me. I was so frustrated but settled down to look for another place to live. One of my friends found us an apartment in the Korntal section of Stuttgart. Korntal was several miles away from the main part of downtown Stuttgart, with smaller homes and more space around the homes. It was a small apartment building, and the apartment was on the first floor. It had a lovely balcony and nice, large, bright rooms. It was the best of the three apartments we had. The large windows in each room let in the sunlight. Both bedrooms were spacious, and we had enough room for our clothes.

My cousin Pavol and his friend came from Slovakia to help us move. What a blessing that turned out to be because they did all the work. We missed our Czech neighbors, but soon they had to move too. I found two German ladies who would come and help with my mother. They only came once a week for one hour, but that was better than no help. My mother looked forward to their visits. They would draw with her or watch TV. They did various activities with her. Eventually, my cousin Pavol and his wife Monica came to stay with us for several months. They were a big help to my mother. They did most of the cooking and cleaning in the apartment. They eventually had to return to Slovakia, and I was once again the main caretaker of my mother. It was six years that she stayed with me, and I was tired because she needed more and more direct care. It was difficult to get full-time care in Germany. I called my sister and told her to find a place in the States for my mother. She consulted with her family doctor, and he recommended a nursing home where he was on the staff. In July of 1994, my mother, my cousin Pavol, and I traveled to Massachusetts to stay with my sister. A nurse came to evaluate my mother and then they said that there was a place for her in the next town at the nursing home.

I said to my mother, "We found a good nursing home near Betty where you would get full-time care."

My mother stated, "I will kill myself before I will go to a nursing home."

With great anxiety, I patiently said, "Maybe you should at least try it and see how you like it."

"I know that I am not going to like it," she replied.

She did go on a trial basis. She never adjusted to it and whenever I visited, she wanted to go home with me. I visited her each day until I had to return to Germany to go back to work. She was now near my sister and my sister would visit her regularly. I would visit each summer for the next seven years. She remained in the nursing home until her death in 2001.

My cousin Pavol and I flew back to Germany feeling sad and exhausted. In the apartment, we felt lonely for my mother. I felt guilty about putting her in a nursing home, but I could not give her the care she needed. She had osteoporosis and had pain most of the time. Even the medications did not ease her pain. In addition, she started having memory problems. She could no longer remember how to sign her name. I would write her name on a piece of paper, and she could copy it. She could not make her own meals and needed help getting dressed. I had to live with the decision to get her more care in a nursing home. Pavol returned to Slovakia, and I felt lonely for him. He was such a help to me in getting my mother to the States and into the nursing home. I was grateful for his help.

A year later, I had to move to Lakenheath, England, due to a job transfer. I didn't want to move again but I had no choice. I worked for the Department of Defense Overseas Schools, which were located on the American bases overseas. When I first started, I was eager to move around in the system. I went to Guantanamo Bay, Cuba, to Misawa, Japan, and then to Yokosuka, Japan. By the time I was in Stuttgart, Germany, I wanted to remain there because I was driving to Zurich, Switzerland, for my Jungian studies. I completed my studies in

Zurich by flying on weekends instead of driving. The principal retired and the new one wanted his own assistant principals, so both my colleague and I were transferred to other schools. I was fortunate that the wife of one of the teachers in Stuttgart who was English agreed to drive with me and helped me get settled in England. She visited her family, who lived in the area. I was the assistant principal at Lakenheath High School, and I was also in charge of the dormitory. The students whose parents were in the military in Saudi Arabia and other places with no American high school lived in the dormitory. I was even able to travel to Saudi Arabia for a week to conduct parent conferences. England turned out to be a good assignment. I rented a row house in West Row, which was not far from the base. I could go to London to see plays and visit museums. I even was able to see Prince Charles, who is now King Charles, at a flower show. I enjoyed the beautiful English gardens. I was in England when Princess Diana was killed in Paris and experienced the great sorrow among the English people. That was a sad time. I visited my mother at Christmas and every summer. I stayed with my sister, but I visited my mother every day while in the States. She was happy to see me, and I would take her outside of the nursing home. She died in 2001 and I no longer went to Massachusetts. After my mother died, I gave more thought to our relationship. What had I missed and what did I not know about her? After reviewing my mother's background and realizing how much she moved around, I had a better understanding of her great anxiety. I don't think I could have survived all the moves she had to make. What were my grandparents thinking when they bounced back and forth between America and Slovakia? I will never understand why my maternal grandmother left her three young daughters with my grandfather in Slovakia and returned to America. My mother and aunt never complained about missing their mother, even when I questioned them. My grandmother's actions are a mystery to me and will always be. My mother never left me and for that I am grateful—at least I don't have a physical abandonment issue. That would have been a great problem for me to work with in therapy.

GRATITUDE

When our days seem dark, it is the time to express gratitude for the blessings we have received in life. My mother did things that I am grateful for. She made sure that I was baptized in the Lutheran Church. She had me attend Sunday School and catechism classes, so I was confirmed. My faith in God and my ties to the Lutheran Church made me feel connected and grounded in more than worldly belongings and collections. My mother was a woman of faith. She served in the church, and she helped many of the immigrant women in the church. A child brought up in faith will build on a solid foundation. If the child as an adult wants to go in a different religious or spiritual direction, then the child has some solid ground to stand on. The daughter is not as easily enticed to follow a false leader or guru. In the fourth commandment, we are admonished to honor our mother and father. To me that means to respect my mother as a human being. It does not mean to accept certain behaviors like excessive mood swings or hysterical outbursts. Those are behaviors that we do not respect, but we still honor the human mother.

Mama wasn't perfect but she was human. She worked hard and set a good example of the ethic of diligent labor for me. She worked all her life for very little pay. I had clean clothes and a roof over my head, and I was never hungry. Mama read stories to me about nature and animals. She drew pictures for me and I learned to draw flowers and enjoy plants. I love having plants to this day. In fact, when I look at my plants both inside and outside, I am energized. The flowers share their energy with me. My mother read fairy tales to me and to this day I appreciate the wisdom of the fairy tale. The Brothers Grimm fairy tale "Snow White and the Seven Dwarfs" was my favorite. I even have a Snow White doll in my doll collection. The dwarfs helped her even when her stepmother's jealousy made her want to destroy Snow White. The stepmother does not identify with her in a positive way. Instead, she allowed her envy of Snow White to dominate her, thus leading her to perform destructive acts toward Snow White. I have found even in my difficult moments God provided an angel to help me in my situation, just as the dwarfs helped Snow White. In looking at my mother's background, her behaviors and attitudes are a natural consequence of the life she lived. Before we judge a person, we need to consider their lives and what contributed to their present behavior and attitudes. According to Dr. Kathrin Asper, "Experience with the mother always leaves its mark on every other form of relationship the adult enters into, whether it be with oneself, other people, things, nature, or, ultimately, with God." There were many people my mother did not like and I often agreed with her to be an obedient daughter. As an adult woman, I had to learn to make my own decisions regarding people, yet some of my mother's comments about people lurked in the back of my mind. I had problems with self-esteem and because I did not value myself, I allowed myself to get in involved in relationships that were not healthy for me.

MOTHER/DAUGHTER RELATIONSHIP

My mother's death led me to ponder the mother/daughter relationship in general. The mother/daughter relationship is very important to the development of a healthy child. A daughter needs a sense of support, warmth, and acceptance from her mother. The young girl can then face the world with a greater sense of security and self-esteem. A young girl learns to become a young woman by the example she experiences from her mother as a model. If the mother dies early or has physical and emotional problems, the young girl needs to find other sources of mothering. It could be a grandmother, aunt, older sister, teacher, or friend. In the fairy tale "Cinderella," the main character has lost her mother to death. She continues to honor her mother by taking a twig to her grave. Unfortunately, the stepmother is not kind to her, but the birds, bees, and godmother step in to take care of her and help her through her difficult times. This is a story of healing. Her helpers remind me of the ram God provided for Abraham so he would not have to sacrifice his son, Isaac. Life always seems to provide some positive intervention. If the mother is too good and too protective, then the daughter has a difficult time in the world. The world has evil people in it and when a daughter has experienced only goodness and kindness, then the evil in the world is a great shock. The daughter has a greater struggle to deal with the evil people and happenings that she encounters in the world. Some difficulties with her mother can be an asset in coping in a world that has evil in it.

A mother's acceptance of her body can also give a daughter a positive image of her body. Acceptance of the body also leads to a sense of self-confidence in the daughter. Emotional acceptance and physical comfort are important in the mother/daughter relationship. Reasonable expectations and positive reinforcement are needed by children. As Dr. Jung states in *Reflections on the Life and Dreams of C. G. Jung* by Aniela Jaffe, "If I did not respond fully to my life's purpose and challenges, then they would be inherited by my children, who would have to bear the burden of my unlived life in addition to their own difficulties." I think a heavy burden was passed on to me by my mother. After I have processed all the hurtful memories, I cannot continue to blame my mother. Behind the personal mother is the ordering and regulating of the archetypes. If the mother/daughter relationship is disturbed, for whatever reason, the negative mother is constellated. As adults, we need to take a look at images and the corresponding archetypes. Effects of being raised by a toxic mother may include higher risk for anxiety and depression. If anxiety and depression are present, it is important to work with a therapist and start looking inward through journaling. Recording and pondering dreams is also helpful and insightful. Kathrin Asper states, "Maternal deprivation, for whatever reason it occurs, is equivalent to a loss of the child's basic sense of herself and inflicts a wound that is difficult to heal." Some mothers, because of their own deprivations, are not able to give their daughters what they need to grow into healthy human beings. The daughter then has to learn to mother herself through self-care, whatever that may be. It is important for the daughter to seek help, so she doesn't repeat the inadequate mothering she received. She can then correct the inadequate mothering she received and do a better job with her own children or other children who look to her for mothering.

When we study fairy tales, we are accessing the wisdom of the ages. Why not use what was given to us? In her book *Interpretation of Fairy Tales*, Marie Louise Von Franz states, "Fairy tales are the purest and simplest expression of collective unconscious psychic processes." Here is where the therapist can help the daughter uncover what is going on in the unconscious regarding the mother/daughter relationship. "The Goose Girl" is a good example of a destructive mother who allows her daughter to go to a strange land and with a wicked servant. The therapist can assist the daughter to see her destructive mother and help her deal with her specific situation constructively. Therapists who work with daughters of difficult mother relationships can gain insights from fairy tales and another one that comes to mind is "Snow White." Reading the fairy tale of Snow White and allowing the insights gained to come to the conscious level can be a real help in the healing process. "The Seven Ravens" and "The Six Swans" teach us that healing a negative mother complex takes time and perseverance. The daughter may be assisted by an animus prince, an image of the unconscious. By responding to the turmoil of the mother complex, one can embrace the task of finding the mother within. With work, the daughter can discover a meaningful and fulfilling life for herself. A fulfilled woman is a good mother for her children and other children who cross her path.

Daughters of immigrant mothers feel the burden of the mother's feeling of inadequacy in the new country, which places an extra burden on the daughter. They may have to accompany the mother to the doctor, dentist, or even to the grocery store. When it comes to paying bills, filing taxes or any other documents, these daughters, even at a young age, have to be in charge of their mother. These daughters often wish their mothers were like their friends' mothers, native to the country. Many resent their mothers and have to work on their anger toward their immigrant mothers. I encourage them to interview their mothers and really understand the mother as a human being. Some daughters find this difficult to do but I suggest that this be done slowly.

According to the Fall 2023 National Council on Family Relations Report, "Worldwide women contribute significantly to the economy through informal work, which has an annual value of $10.8 trillion; this work entails a staggering 12.5 billion hours of unpaid labor daily." The care of mothers falls mainly to the daughters, and if there are no daughters, the wives of sons play a key role in elder care. Many daughters have had to put their careers on hold to care for a mother. Even if the daughter places the mother in a nursing home, they still have a lot of responsibility. Daughters need to look at their relationships with their mothers and plan what role they will play in the mother's elder care.

COVID-19 created increased burdens on daughters caring for mothers. They had difficulty getting help because caregivers were scarce, so at times self-care activities were put aside. Working women had to take time off from their jobs to care for their mothers. Taking time off from work did not help women who were seeking promotions.

It took me a long time to really understand my mother and to stop judging her. When she came to live with me in Stuttgart, I tried to interview her about her childhood and her early life. This is when I learned how much Michigan meant to her. Whenever someone mentioned Michigan or she heard it on the TV, her eyes lit up and she transported herself back to Michigan. I sometimes wish we had taken a trip back to Michigan and shared memories of the place. I would sit down and color with her because I know she enjoyed the coloring books we purchased together. She was so proud that she could color one page, as if she had produced a da Vinci drawing. Through my years of therapy, I was able to work out my issues with my mother. One therapist said to me, "Can't you forgive your mother?" That statement really woke me up. Working with forgiving and understanding my mother helped me to better understand the clients I see who have mother problems. I have greater empathy for them and yet I encourage them to move ahead with their lives. It is important for me to provide an accepting and warm environment for my clients to assist in their healing process.

MAMA'S FINAL HOME
IN MASSACHUSETTS

My mother went into the nursing home on foot but ended up in a wheelchair in her last years. My sister called the nursing home "death's waiting room." My mother tolerated the nursing home, but she was never happy there. Whenever I would visit, she would beg me to take her home with me. It saddened me to leave her and I would often cry after I left, but I could not care for her by myself. On her eightieth birthday, my sister, niece, nephew, and I celebrated with her. She was dressed in light blue pants and a matching top. The outfit made her look younger. We bought her a rose corsage and a small vanilla and chocolate cake. She seemed happy to see all of us but tears came when we had to leave. I prayed that I would never have to go into a nursing home because I saw how unhappy my mother was there. At least she was clean and safe, but that does not seem like enough. The nursing home had a lovely dining area for the residents, but my mother did not want to go there. She had her meals brought to her room, where she ate alone in peace and quiet. Although my mother was a social person, she did not participate in any of the home's events. She did not know any of the people in the home and she was reluctant to engage in conversations with them. She did like a few of the staff members and talked with them. That was her only socialization. When I would visit, I would put her in a wheelchair, and we would go outside. I would push her around and point out all the beautiful flowers. She would enjoy seeing the flowers and being outside.

My mother survived in the nursing home for seven years. How she did that in a place that she did not like was a miracle to me. She had good survival skills and I guess all her earlier moves in life helped her develop them. Perhaps my visits and my sister's visits kept her going over the years. If family is involved in a person's nursing home care, it makes a difference in the care and survival of the patient. There are patients whose families dump them in a nursing home and never visit. These patients really suffer from feelings of being abandoned. That is why my sister and I were careful to place her in a home near one of us. My sister's doctor was also on the staff of the home and that made a difference in my mother's medical care. Choosing the right home for a person is very important for the care of the person. At times one may have to move a person from one home to a better facility for that person. We were fortunate that this home was the best choice for my mother. My sister was with her just before she died and then made all the arrangements for her final resting place. I was grateful that my sister took the responsibility for doing that. My mother went from the nursing home to the church triumphant, which means that she is with God. I believe that she is at peace.

FINAL THOUGHTS

Perhaps my mother felt abandoned by me as she had been by her mother. Abandonment by a mother is difficult for a woman to bear. Without therapeutic intervention, which my mother never had, life is difficult. In her book, Kathrin Asper writes, "A child experiences herself as abandoned primarily when her feelings are not noticed and understood with empathy by someone else, particularly the mother." In my mother's situation, her mother was not available to notice and understand her feelings. My mother moved from Michigan to Slovakia to New York City to Maryland and back to New York City. In New York City, we lived in four different places. After New York City, she moved to Stuttgart, Germany, and then to the nursing home in Massachusetts. I too moved around in my life, but my moves were my choice and my mother's moves were not her choice. I think that she felt that things just happened to her, and she had no power over anything. Knowing my mother's background and her issues helped me better understand her. As a child, I had no idea what was behind her actions. Yet, even though my mother was damaged, she raised a successful daughter. I graduated from college with a BA in history and taught high school English and social studies. I was the first one in my family to obtain a college degree. In addition, I obtained two master's degrees and a doctorate in education. While teaching, I attended the Jung Institute in Zurich and completed a diploma in analytical psychology. I have been blessed to follow my own life journey. Writing this book has helped me better understand my mother and her complex nature. I encourage others with mother problems to look beyond the surface to understand the dynamics. It is important to get help to resolve the issues within yourself so that personal goals are achieved despite family dynamics.

PHOTOS

Brass Factory in Muskegon Heights, Michigan.

On the left is my mother Anna, and on the right is her sister Susie. My grandfather is holding their sister, Kristina.

Vrbovce, Slovakia.

Vrbovce, Slovakia.

Vrbovce, Slovakia.

Pictured here is my mother.

This is my mother and my grandmother, Anna.

This was my parents' wedding in 1936.

My parents.

My mother dressed in her Slovak costume.

Me and my mother.

Bata Shoe Factory in Belcamp, Maryland.

My mother at age seventy-seven.

My mother, sister Betty, and me.

Zuzana's doll house, 2024.

ACKNOWLEDGMENTS

PAMELA MCDONALD,
who helped me fix up my doll house for filming and pictures.

GRACE SCOFIELD,
who typed and corrected my manuscript.

NOAH SCOFIELD,
who videoed my doll house and fixed my printer.

MARLENE HOCHMAN,
director of the Toy Museum of New York, helped
me find a purpose for my doll collection.

BERNICE HORNAK SAND,
who has been my childhood friend and a good listener.

LINDA SMITH AND JIM RECTOR,
who support my creative endeavors and ideas.

PEARL VINCES,
who is my cousin and shared the information
regarding my maternal grandfather's work at the
Brass Factory in Michigan.

RALPH ROBERT HENSON,
who listened to my stories of my relationship
with my mother.

All the people at ATMOSPHERE PRESS,
who made this book a reality.

"Where I have been unable to remember fully, I have
allowed my imagination to fill in."

ABOUT ATMOSPHERE PRESS

Founded in 2015, Atmosphere Press was built on the principles of Honesty, Transparency, Professionalism, Kindness, and Making Your Book Awesome. As an ethical and author-friendly hybrid press, we stay true to that founding mission today.

If you're a reader, enter our giveaway for a free book here:

SCAN TO ENTER
BOOK GIVEAWAY

If you're a writer, submit your manuscript for consideration here:

SCAN TO SUBMIT
MANUSCRIPT

And always feel free to visit Atmosphere Press and our authors online at atmospherepress.com. See you there soon!

AUTHOR BIOGRAPHY

ZUZANA PLESA has a doctorate in education, which she earned at the University of West Florida, Pensacola. She has two master's degrees, one from Fuller Seminary in Pasadena, California, and the other from Hofstra University in New York. She earned her bachelor's degree from Wagner College in Staten Island, New York. She is a licensed marriage and family therapist and a Zurich-trained Jungian Analyst. After retiring from the Department of Defense Overseas School where she worked as a teacher, counselor, and administrator, she moved to Florida. She counsels active duty military members and their families.

Milton Keynes UK
Ingram Content Group UK Ltd.
UKHW040815051024
449151UK00004B/226